My Words

I did not have to power to speak and so I wrote.

Belle Doyle

To my father for giving me my love of literature.

To my mother for loving and supporting everything I do.

Contents:

(not by page number, merely the order)

Intro:

1. A Butterfly and a Semicolon
2. Pour My Soul
3. Work Missions
4. Manic Mind
5. Rhyme
6. Escapism
7. You Shall Never
8. Sky on Fire
9. Well of Poems

Part 1: Seedling

1. Witches' Blood
2. Dead an Hour
3. Perception
4. Protect Your Peace
5. Jester
6. Rock of Ridicule
7. Ice Age
8. Survive
9. I Cannot Stand You
10. The Diary Friend
11. Fade Away
12. Disconnected
13. Two Years
14. Little Monkey's Secret
15. Wake Up

16. Deserved Death
17. Dance of Drowning
18. Whirlwind Mind
19. Dread Filled Head
20. Tethers
21. Wolves
22. Shambles
23. Abandonment
24. Dying Light
25. Realization
26. Night of Delirium
27. Your Gods
28. Devils Side
29. Relationships
30. The Selfish Obtuse
31. Marathon of Burdens
32. Two Weeks
33. Free my soul
34. No Reason
35. Tug of war
36. Incurable
37. I'll go first

Part 2: Blooming

1. Throne
2. Bow
3. Self-Reliance
4. It's Time to Grow
5. Demon Eyes
6. World of Roses
7. Brothers Love
8. Moon Girl
9. Other Girls
10. Fathers

11. Intuition

12. Recipe for Solace

13. Coming Home

14. Compressional Societal Expectations

15. Save Yourself

16. Red-eyed Girl

17. Wild Mind

18. Deserved

19. Impact

20. Inside Out

21. How the Mighty Fall

22. Immortal

23. Repetition of Trauma

24. Yesterdays, Tomorrows, and Today

25. Born or Made

Part 3: Spreading growth

1. Empty Gods

2. Memento Mori

3. Run Boy

4. Run Girl

5. Pyres

6. Subconscious Hauntings

7. Influence Yourself

8. Addict

9. Flatline

10. They're Coming for You

11. Flowers

12. People are Ugly

13. Seek Out

14. Innocence

15. Welcoming Death

16. Puzzled Hurricane

17. Letters to Men

18. Effect of Words

Introduction:

A Butterfly and a Semicolon

The girl that says,
"I know"
When you tell her of heartbreak
"I know"
When you tell her of deceit
"I know"
When you tell her of exhaustion
"I know"
When you to tell her of family strife
"I know"
When you tell her of depression
"I know"
When you tell her of battle scars
Is the girl that survived it all,
And walked away with
A butterfly and a semicolon.
- Belle Doyle (5)

Pour My Soul

Why must every poetry configuration
Be about mental conceptions?
Is there not more to explore?
If one drowns within their pain
In such explicit ways
Will they ever be saved?
Or will they simply exist in a world
Of pain and anguish?
No. This cannot be.
Life blooms and grows as all should.
One may say that to
Pour their souls darkness
Into darkness
Is to cure
But is this a façade by the witching hour?
As I pour my soul into these
Words
I gaze at 3:33am and realize
I too have been
Tricked.
- Belle Doyle (9)

Work's Missions

There are two sides
To the reason I write.
The first is rather selfish;
For the burn in my hand
As it races across the page,
Trying to keep in time
With the pace of my mind:
Is a healing unparalleled
To all else.
The second reason
Is for those
Drowning with nothing to grasp
And no belief they can write
Words of their own,
I hope to create
Page upon page
They can grab hold of
And find a solace
So curing and whole
They just may
Breathe again.
- Belle Doyle (144)

Manic Mind

11:16pm
Words fill my mind
My pen strains to keep in time,
As line by line flies by.
It begins to sweat as another
Title flutters to life
With a new theme,
And a new emotion
That would change the one
Racing to be written.
11:18pm
This pen sweats and swears,
It seems as though time is crawling
While it is fiercely running.
It chases word after word
Until...
One slips away
Just the right word to fly,
To end this train
In
Its
Tracks.
What was that idea?
What was that word?
What was that line?
11:20pm
I cannot think
Anymore.
This pen

Collapses.
And the words within this manic mind
Flee
As if called to another.
- Belle Doyle (25)

Rhyme

Where people misunderstand
With poetry
Is that it does not
Need to rhyme.
Poems should heal.
Either they should
Heal the poets heart
And ruin the readers,
Or ruin the poets
And heal the reader.
For life and its tragedies
Are not cohesive,
So why should your words be?
- Belle Doyle (49)

Escapism

Unwittingly she dived,
She dived into fantastical worlds
Where the line of life and death
Is danced upon with glee.
She dived into a world
Where steel swords replaced
Diamonds as a girl's best friend.
She dived where
Ghouls, goblins, and gorgons
Taunted your every step,
Though she dived where
Family was cherished
Like the moon by the Earth
And she needn't worry
About the
Drakes, dragons, and dryads.
She dived into worlds
Of sky-high marble
And blood drenched fields
Where war was unyielding.
She dived deeper and deeper
Until her own name
Was lost amidst siren songs.
She dived into a world
Where she had
Bravery and beauty.
A gust of wind
Ripped through pristine papers
And tore her away

From worlds of wonder.
She found herself
Back in a field of dandelion
She knew she could not
Escape.
- Belle Doyle (6)

You Shall Never

You shall never see me cry
Yet it's evidence lay
Within my every cursive line.
You shall never see me beg
Yet my pleads lay
Within my every scribble and swoop.
You shall never see me cheer
With pure undiluted joy,
Yet its evidence lay
Within my every press and print.
You shall never see me
For who I am
If you never crack
The spine
Of endless words
My mouth could never speak.
- Belle Doyle (162)

Sky On Fire

The sky is on fire
But no one seems to mind.
Rather they take pictures
And say
"Isn't it pretty?"
Shouldn't we be concerned?
Red, yellow, and orange
Dance to the sound
Of our demise.
"Our sky is on fire!
How do you only see the beauty?"
"Oh, little overthinker, it is merely
Sunset."
- Belle Doyle (53)

Well of Poems

Oh, endless well,
Oh, endless well,
What should I write today?
You offer me too much, I say.
Oh, well of fortune,
Oh, well of hope,
Oh, well of nature,
Oh, well of joy,
Oh, well of solitude.
No not right, I say.
Oh, endless well,
Oh, endless well,
What should I write today?
You offer me too much, I say.
Oh, well of despair,
Oh, well of depression,
Oh, well of destruction,
Oh, well of anger,
Oh, well of isolation.
No not right, I say.
Nothing comes to my pen.
It seems as though
Great well,
You have failed me
Today.
- Belle Doyle (55)

Part 1:
Seedling

Witches' Blood

I do not believe these veins
Run blue blood
As a witch's veins do.
For even when burning,
A witch never stops fighting.
I try dearly
To share their fiery,
But when the flames of
Depression,
Anxiety,
And self-hatred
Rose high,
I stop.
I stop and let them.
Even as
Smoke climbs in my nose,
And flames lick my fingertips,
I stop fighting,
And my hands slacken.
I even fan the flames,
When they reach my parched lips.
But I forget...
That witches did not stop
Because they did not
Need too.
They are magic after all.
I am not.
I am human.
I cannot fight with

Every fiber of my being
Till the end of days.
I forget that
It is okay
To stop
And
Breathe
As long as you
Keep fighting;
- Belle Doyle (42)

Dead An Hour

I'd been dead only an hour.
Initially I felt relief,
For nothing had caught up yet.
I savoured,
Basked,
Loved my new-found,
All consuming darkness
That was to be my new home.
I felt no pain,
No fear,
But also no joy in the dark.
Then suddenly,
As fast as tripping over
The lip of a rug,
It all came back.
I missed my family,
My father's warm laugh,
My mother's comfort,
My brothers' unique love.
I missed all I had yet to do,
And all I could not resolve.
I yearned for pen and paper,
But my ghastly fingers
Met nothing but open air.
The worst of all?
All the pain I tried to escape,
Rushed back with
A vengeance.
But this time

I had nothing and no one
To ease the endless ache.
I'd been dead only an hour,
And realized,
I'd rather
Live.
- Belle Doyle (69)

Perception

Isn't perception a beautiful thing?
I adore the moon and its company,
But you believe it bland
And instead seek the sun.
I admired a wildflower and left it be,
But you took a thistle saying
"I can fix it."
You believed yourself
To be the hero
But I knew you to be
The villain.
- Belle Doyle (77)

Protect Your Peace

Remember to protect your peace.
Remember to protect your peace
From those who wish to
Steal your glory,
Rob your justice,
Take your happiness,
Break your sanity,
Cheat you of revenge,
Sabotage your satisfaction
All behind pretty smiles
And endearing words.
Remember to protect your peace...
But not so thoroughly
As to leave you
Completely,
Entirely,
And utterly,
Alone.
- Belle Doyle (86)

Jester

In my meadow,
I sit,
Alone and at peace.
You saunter in,
With an air
of ease and ego.
I see your
Bruises and scratches
And laugh with little heart,
For I know they were earned
From the feat of
Entering my golden garden of seclusion.
I laugh at your stark pride,
Knowing your battle has
Barely begun.
You creep closer.
I lay my head against
My log of serenity,
In welcome to your
Unnecessary attempts.
You try to peer into my soul
Through pathetic small talk.
I wait in amused silence,
As you attempt at
Inclusion,
Conversation,
Connection,
Even bribery
To break through

The pure iron chains
Around my heart,
Locked by a
Long-lost key.
You try everything
And anything.
How truly adorably amusing.
Though all good things
Must end,
As your eyes darken,
And your desire dims.
I decide to throw a bone,
For I am not yet
Tired of
My jester.
I stand and engage
Your dry company.
The gears of interaction
Within my mind
Click to life.
You jump in glee
For you believed
It was the chains
Around my heart
Falling away,
How silly of you.
I continue to play along
Like a father covered in makeup
With their five-year-old daughter.
You believe you have
Finally convinced me
Of friendship,
Yet I still believe you to be
A staggering stranger.
I wonder how you cannot

Interpret the vast sea of a foot
Between us.
Still on a high of achievement,
You race from my meadow,
And into the surrounding thick-thorned lush,
Believing me in tow,
Though you do not bother a glance back.
I laugh once more,
For you fled without glancing at my feet,
Tied in the bramble of my log of serenity,
Forbidding me of fleeing,
Even if I dare dream too.
A smirk dances upon my lips
As I sit among billowing blades of grass
And tranquil tulips,
As I gather my pen and paper,
And write of our inconsequential interaction,
With the dying light
Of sunset.
When the stream of words
Drizzle to a trickle,
And the moon stares down,
I lay my head against
My log of serenity
Once more,
And await another
Jester
To fool.
- Belle Doyle (99)

Rock of Ridicule

You take the same walk
Each day,
And each day,
You trip and stumble
Over the same
Rock.
Each day you
Step in the same spot,
Step on the same rock's
Sharp head,
And down you go.
You scrape your palms to the point,
They do not bother to heal.
You continue to return
To what hurts you
Day by day
Almost as though
You could not survive
Without the
Pain.
- Belle Doyle (102)

Ice Age

My girl your soft brown eyes
Have seemed to have
Frozen over.
What has happened?
My girl your eyes
Have lost the depth
Of earth brown
That held the power
To bring cities to cinders
And the confidence to make
Mountains bow down.
Where has it all gone?
My girl your eyes
Have lost their
Friendly gaze
That any creature
Could make a home.
They've lost the freedom to
Grow and change
Without any fear of external pry.
Who did this to you?
"My poor girl" A reflection
The past says in pity
To its aged stare
So cold,
The reflection could not believe
They were one
And the same.

- Belle Doyle (127)

Survive

I once wished for people
To silent their automated messages
To my "I'm not okay"
But when someone tells me of their
Life's trife,
I find myself doing the
Exact same thing
I dread hearing most.
I realize then,
That I do not have
The energy to spare
And maybe
Whoever I have tried
To reach out to,
Is doing the same;
Saving their energy
To survive.
Isn't that our most primal instinct?
Thousands of feet above ground
And yet
You put your mask on
Before anyone else,
In that
Plummeting promise
Of death.
Oh, there's so much more,
And I ask myself
What right do I have
To ask anyone

To put me before you?
- Belle Doyle (107)

25

I Cannot Stand You

I cannot stand you
And all you do.
You say
"I'm a hero."
Yet my pain falls on deaf ears.
I cannot stand you
And all you do.
You say
"This is all your fault."
But do you not see
What you've done?
I cannot stand you
And all you do.
You say
"I'll be there soon."
But it's five hours later
And you're nowhere
To be found.
I cannot stand you
And all of you.
For I stand alone once more
And all of you
Have vanished
Into true colours.
- *Belle Doyle (115)*

The Diary Friend

"How are you?" I ask.
Her mouth overflows with
Adventure and splendor.
She tells me of her
Fun with friends.
She tells me of her
Family and their insanity.
I listen and listen...
The weight of my life
Bear down upon my shoulders
Begging to be lifted
By a simple
"How are you?"
- Belle Doyle (1)

Fade Away

Why would I continue to stay,
When you never noticed me
Fading away
When
Leaves began to
Seek the sun,
When
Ice and snow
Screamed under the sun's
Heating glare.
Now the ice and snow
Laugh at the sun's
Sour attempts to melt away
Their fresh layer of wilting white.
And I fear for you,
Fear you have lost me forever,
As I
Fade
Away.
- Belle Doyle (8)

Disconnected

Words on a page
Show love and lust
As adamant and sure,
Show any pure feeling
As certain and within
The grasp of their fingertips.
But when I see a
Lovely girl
I could see myself with,
A girl
With a fluent heart and shocking words;
I feel as if I like her.
That loose screw in my trust
Falls away,
And knocks a cord
Barely balancing,
To connect any
Inclination for intimacy
To my tornado mind.
Suddenly,
There's no flecks of
Gold in her earthy eyes.
Suddenly,
Her voice squeaks
And my ears quiver.
Suddenly,
Her hair is flat
And lost its life.
Suddenly,

I feel as though
I'd never felt that fondness.
A fondness that floats away
Like a poorly tied boat
On a high tide.
My imposter feet carry me past
The girl of my dreams
I turned into a nightmare,
All in a matter
Of moments.
- Belle Doyle (126)

Two Years

Two years clean,
And yet it feels like yesterday.
Two years clean,
And yet it haunts me
Like a growing shadow at dusk.
Two years clean,
And yet I somehow
Feel the same.
Two years clean,
And yet somehow
I feel completely anew.
Two years clean,
Since a sliver pen
Danced upon skin
Spilling red ink.
Two years clean,
But am I
Any different than
Before?
- Belle Doyle (170)

Little Monkey's Secret

"Look at that little monkey,"
They'd all say,
As she went by.
"Look at that little monkey,"
They'd all say,
As she swung from
Branch to branch
With such freedom and ease.
"Look at that little monkey."
They'd all say,
As she climbed
Any high tree
She saw.
"Look at that little monkey,
I wonder what she'll do next."
And with that
The monkey knew
She'd fooled them all.
For she never climbed a tree
She hadn't before,
She never touched a branch,
That she did not already
Trust it's bristled bark
To not snap,
She never went beyond the leaves
She knew well
To venture
Into an unknown
She could not

Control.
- Belle Doyle (132)

WAKE UP

Grey brick winding road
It's pitch black all around
But your faces are all so clear.
When I reach you
We hug and talk
And when our interaction reaches it's close,
You lean in and say,
"Wake up"
The farther I go the more urgent
You all get.
What's the hurry?
Don't you find this darkness as
Comforting as I?
When I reach you,
Mercedes,
I do not recognize you immediately,
Though my soul cries
In a life we could've had.
You're merely a shadowed outline
Of long hair and a battered dress;
A sister I'd never know.
You spare no time for empathy,
Nor connection.
You do not even bother a hello,
Though this may be the only time
We meet,
You grab my arms and rattle me
To my very bones
With your ghastly grasp.

You beg and plead.
I don't understand... Why?
The only words you shout
Again and again,
"WAKE UP"
- Belle Doyle (157)

Deserved Death

After all that happened,
And all that's been accomplished,
And all the dreams left to be achieved,
I hoped,
Once all said and done,
I hoped for a bright ending,
Knowing that could mean
Crashing,
And
Burning.
And
Drowning,
As painfully
As the voice in the
Corner of my mind
Whispers
I deserve.
- Belle Doyle (145)

Dance of Drowning

I say I hate
Water's deep blues,
Say I hate
It's suffocating silk,
Say I hate
The unknown of what
Lurks in the black,
Say I hate
It's crushing weight.
I say I hate
The feeling of drowning
In mental turmoil
And yet
As soon as
My quivering hands
Reach the sandy shore,
I plunge back
Into the crushing depths.
After swimming
With your demons
For so long,
You're feet forget,
How to take a step.
It becomes all you know
To dance with darkness
And feel
Betrayed
By the light.
- Belle Doyle (149)

Whirlwind Mind

You've all left and
Though I cannot fault you
For we all have lives to carry out
And who am I to wish for you to stay
But
I do any-who.
For when the silence begins to
Ring in warning
I barely raise my sword in time
Before demons
Attack me from all sides.
It's violent mayhem.
What am I to do?
I can't breathe
My legs can't move,
My lips are sealed,
My body quivers,
And my eyes water
From the turmoil
I cannot control.
The cycle is repeating,
But who knows,
If I shall survive
This round of my
Whirlwind mind.
- Belle Doyle (151)

Dread-filled head

It doesn't feel real.
The time does not feel
Like enough.
The bell shall toll
And I dread the next
Turn of the tide
For the lies spun and
The unnecessary weight
Placed upon my shoulders
With my own
Self-loathing fingers.
Will it be too much?
Will I crumble?
Or will I thrive?
Can't turn back now
The ball has begun to roll,
Round and round.
The fire has begun to blaze
Higher and higher.
Only time shall tell
If they will make it to
The finish line.
Heart sputters in
Anxious anticipation.
Will the clock ever toll?
To say my dream came true
And I shall fall to bits?
Or will it say
I must follow suit with

The dull mass in prerequisite ritual?
I dread the next
Turn of the tide and all
It shall tell,
And yet,
I cannot await it's
Cool, heartbreaking,
Splash of woe.
- Belle Doyle (159)

Tethers

So few tethers tie me to
The stake of life.
The knowledge of the pain
That shall haunt my mothers
Every heartbeat,
Should I lay in peace
Six feet below,
Keeps me tethered.
The knowledge I shall never say
"Look at me now,"
To all who inadvertently
Lay scars upon my skin
And to my own enemy hand,
Keeps me tethered.
I for one,
Cannot stand to fail,
No matter how small a trip,
Or how big a stumble,
My mind beats itself to a pulp.
The knowledge I would
Fail
Simply at living,
Keeps me tethered
To the stake of life.

- Belle Doyle (161)

Wolves

Hungry,
Prowling beasts
Of past,
Present,
And future
Gathering round and surrounding
A mind on the brink of despair
Hoping to be the one to send
It over the edge.
They take turns
Biting and attacking,
Fresh flesh,
That simply begs
To sleep
Amid chaos
Only it can control
And yet does not realize
The wolves are at it's
Mercy.
- Belle Doyle (172)

Shambles

I hate the implication
That all poet's
Are healing from those
Who broke their hearts.
For mine is perfectly whole...
It is my mind rather
That is in
Shambles.
- Belle Doyle (57)

Abandonment

Houses get abandoned,
Pets get abandoned,
Instruments get abandoned,
Work gets abandoned,
Goals get abandoned,
Traditions get abandoned.
But I,
Have abandoned
Your heart.
- Belle Doyle (61)

Dying Light

There is no one left
To witness
The dwindling soul,
Sitting in the dark
With only the moon for comfort.
Someone emerges.
"Oh be my company! Enjoy my light!"
The light sputters to life
And dances in the hopes of an onlooker.
But instead, the onlooker
Rains down, killing it's glee,
Leaving the dying campfire
Alone,
In this dark night
With nothing but a
Small flicker of delight.
- Belle Doyle (63)

Realization

Stuck in an endless war,
Drowning,
Yet somehow thriving.
Craving for company,
Yet distrust clogs my throat.
I love my quiet,
But there's a point
One needs more.
Many have tried to climb
These walls,
Adorned with life
To make them believe
They were inside.
My anxiety coos
That this is what's right,
But realization is beginning to strike,
That it is not.
Yet I still sit with a pleasant smile
Outside a circle
Of secure people.
- Belle Doyle (81)

Night of Delirium

10:30pm
Begin to wind down.
Mind is whole,
Reality is one and dream another.
11:30pm
Collapse into billowing fabrics.
Mind is whole,
But reality takes a backseat
As sleep takes hold.
Eyes slide closed.
1:34am
Eyes fly open.
It's not real, just a dream.
Mind frays.
Reality and dream begin to meld.
Reality holds for but a moment,
And eyes slide closed into
A land of mischief and mayhem.
3:38am
Eyes flutter open once more.
Mismatched dreams and memories
Dance in confusing glee.
One misstep...
And free falling...
Darkness is all the eye can see.
4:26am
Lightning skitters upon nerves,
Body bolts upright,
Panting breaths,

Reality snaps into place.
- Belle Doyle (89)

Your Gods

Some believe their
High chins and prying fingers,
Will walk through
Golden gates
And be greeted
By a man with a plan,
When their souls are reaped.
Believe those who do not
Follow their interpretation
Of rules from long lost words,
Are doomed to a hell
Ruled by a fallen angel,
Who too, disregarded the rules
Made by the man with a plan:
God himself.
This cannot be in my mind.
For how can one being rule all?
Control all?
See all?
Help all?
Need all?
Doom all?
There cannot be just one
For us all,
For if there was,
How cruel he is.
Give some glory
And others,
Pure condemnation.

49

Some riches,
And some a crumb.
Is it a game?
Give some a long healthy life,
And steal others
After six hours.
Free some of torturous demons,
Only to give them to another.
You say it's balance,
I say it's his gamble.
Make some strong and abusive,
set on destruction,
And another ill-equipped to the
First's tyranny.
Flood towns in
Water, wine, and blood.
Never give one a break,
Let the other never know the need.
You say he has his reasons,
But what are they then?
If your god is so kind,
Why did he give me
A mind like this?
Some believe there are numerous gods.
One for war.
One for peace.
One for life.
One for death.
One for the harvest.
One for spring.
One for love and beauty.
One for mischief and chaos.
One for bravery and valor.
One for the moon.
One for the sun.

One for anything you can think.
And yet...
How do they not see
Anyone with a breath
To spare on a prayer?
I believe in neither of your gods.
So when you ask what awaits
Me after my final demise,
I say I do not know,
But hopefully I do not
Have to start again,
As so many say
I may.
- *Belle Doyle (96)*

Devil's Side

There's a saying
"The villain will always be
The villain if the
Hero tells the story."
So I ask...
What is the
Devil's side?
The first evil
To dare 'good'.
The ultimate sinner.
The one all should fear.
Yet I wonder,
If he is so terrible,
Why would he punish
His own kind?
- *Belle Doyle (101)*

Relationships

I do not understand
How you cry a river
When they inevitable leave,
When they show their true colours
You refused to acknowledge
All along.
I do not understand how you may
Lay yourself bare
To their will and act surprised
When they betray your heart.
I do not understand
How you cry a river,
For I refuse to ever
Let myself be loved
So entirely and
Let myself be so vulnerable
To one
I cannot predict.
Maybe I'm simply too young
To understand,
And yet
What a shame
To already feel
So far
Gone.
- Belle Doyle (118)

The Selfish Obtuse

Oh spoiled
Little brat,
Who on this dying planet
Let you believe it is okay
To write off
Your insolence,
Harm,
And audacity
Towards your familiars
On your bad day?
Morals and maturity
Do not fall away
With the drop of your tear.
- Belle Doyle (125)

Marathon of Burdens

Oh how dangerous of you
To ask for my shoes.
They slip on with misguided ease,
And off you go.
You say the first mile
Was cheerful
But ordinarily boring.
The second and third
You began to understand
Why I say "I can't"
To most plans.
On the fourth mile,
The thirst for validation
Wrapped around your bones
To the point a percentage
Determined your worth.
The fifth and sixth
Your nose involuntarily greets the sky,
In the presence of your peers
Doing just what they should,
And suddenly you are
Cozy under your covers
By 9:30pm on Friday.
On the seventh and eight
You were bombarded by my memories
And my demons
Tried to drag you back
Two years.
My few angels fought to

Keep you present.
On the ninth
Comparison entered the tug of war
And yanked your chin high.
You walked,
And walked,
Being beaten and pulled apart
By invisible burdens
You tried dearly to hide behind pleasantries.
When you returned,
You had no words to say,
You were tattered
And shell-shocked.
You slipped away once more,
As everyone has
And I slipped
My shoes back on
Knowing only I
Could fill them.
- Belle Doyle (109)

Two Weeks

I have not written in
Two weeks.
What is wrong with me?
I have not written in
Two weeks.
I miss my pen
And the flow of words.
I have not written in
Two weeks.
In two weeks
I've cried myself to sleep,
Been torn
Between two
Vastly different souls,
Felt pride,
Felt pain,
Felt joy,
Yet I have not written in
Two weeks.
- Belle Doyle (174)

Free My Soul

It has gotten to the point again,
When the littlest things
Set my eyes burning,
Yet my voice says
"I'm okay"
Though the rain
That started a hurricane,
Rages behind this still voice.
A hand reaches through the fog,
And I cringe away and say
"I'm fine"
Though this time, the hand persists.
2020 begs for me
To return,
But this time,
I take the hand.
This time my mouth
Speaks as it has not spoken
For those who do not share my roof.
They listen and offer comfort where needed.
And though my words weren't right and
barely scratched the
Surface of turmoil,
My soul felt freedom in those
Short minutes,
That I wish I could extend.
Though this hurricane
Is yet to settle,
The rain has lessened.

Maybe if this is the beginning
Of a new habit,
Rather than any dangerous and frightening
Old habits,
The ones that lead to a semicolon,
I will do enough to
Free my soul,
To ease it's
Tries, trifes, tribulations,
And trust issues.
Oh I hope
This step shall do the trick.
You say I have a
Long life ahead of me
But if history repeats,
Will that be true?
Shall my soul free?
- *Belle Doyle (50)*

No Reason

Sorrow rests deep
In these bones.
Anxiety replaces skin
As deep as an artery.
Sorrow climbs my spine
Reaching and climbing
Until it meets my brain
And poisons
Rich optimistic red
To dead pessimistic black.
It's dark but the lights are on.
Surrounded by people
But so alone.
There's no more reason.
Sorrow no longer simply rests,
As the light flickers out.
- Belle Doyle (178)

Tug of War

It's a war zone
Won't you believe?
This heart lay in
Long forgotten shreds,
Tugged and torn
Between
Survival and succumb.
It's a war zone
Won't you believe?
Stoic, unyielding face
Bullets ricochet
It's all so loud
It's all so feared.
It's a war zone
Won't you believe?
Succumb pleads promises
Survival has gone quiet.
You all can't see
Even when this shredded heart
Is laid bare
Right in front of your eye.
It's a war zone
Won't you believe?
Who's going to win?
It's hard to tell
Even as will
Walks off the
Blood drenched field.
It's a war zone

Won't you believe?
It's raged for years
Beneath a tear stained eye.
Your all so blind,
I say.
It's a war zone
Won't you believe?
A dangerous war locked behind
Obsidian walls
For wouldn't you say
Their war
Is in much more
Peril?
It's a war zone
I believe.
It's a war all in my mind
And I wonder
How do you not see?
And yet there I sit
With a smile,
Eyes somehow bright,
Voice somehow strong.
Yet there I sit
Wondering how
You do not see
When I do not show
A single hint
For your blind eye.
- Belle Doyle (175)

Incurable

How sad... I think
As her back
Is all I see.
How sad... I think
She could not last
To be so
Impossibly far
Under the
Veil of intimacy.
How sad... I think
My mind ruined another chance
That hadn't even formed.
- Belle Doyle (177)

I'll Go First

Ten years
Of raw undiluted,
Love-filled,
Heartbreaking,
Dedication
To never get a goodbye.
To not be chosen
Over a witch.
Two years
Of kindness
Laughter,
Sisterhood,
To slip away
Through my fingers
And to never get a goodbye.
Oh I knew this one was
Temporary,
Yet didn't the memories
Warrant a goodbye?
A year and a half
I believe.
Two summers to say,
Sisterhood,
Sincerity,
Horseplay
And yet
That fateful day
At the dusk of a fortnight
You marched off

To never give a goodbye.
Today you stand before me,
You started this
And I knew you'd leave.
But my, your eyes,
A brown so rich
I could drown.
And I am.
I knew.
I knew.
I knew you'd leave too.
But my your voice,
A sirens song
To drag me to depths unknown
I felt like a
Self-destructive adventure.
I knew.
I knew.
I knew you'd leave too.
Today you stand so much
Farther than before.
You haven't left yet...
But won't you?
I'll save you the heartache,
I'll save you the tears,
I'll save you the connection,
I'll go first.
I'll leave without a goodbye.
As though we'd
Never
Met.
- Belle Doyle (180)

Part 2:
Blooming

Throne

God upon god
Ignored her tiny violin
Even as she played
Louder
And
Louder,
To no avail.
They turned a blind eye,
Until she too,
Turned her back upon the Gods
And toward the only being
Who took pity...
The devil.
The devil came to teach her
To shape her violin bow
Into a sword to
Cut down her pain and disdain
Into a throne.
- Belle Doyle (94)

Bow

A bow must first pull back
Before shooting forward.
But you seem to have missed the message.
You pound your pain
Deeper and deeper
Then grovel for a victory
That will never arrive.
Your disregarded demons
Laugh and lug
The finish line
From your seizing hands.
You wish to plow forward
As if you were
An emotionless bull.
Forgetting your mind
Is tethered to the past.
Breathe and remember,
To step back is to move forward.
- Belle Doyle (29)

Self-Reliance

I was dying,
Waiting for someone else's words
I wouldn't hear any-who,
Forgetting
My words are just
As powerful
And rose from the
Depths of despair
On steps of self-reliance.
- Belle Doyle (31)

It's Time to Grow

Dear self and everyone like you,
Stop wasting time
Gazing at the moon
Wondering about what if's,
For eventually the moon
Will set
And the sun
Will rise
And if you cling solely
To what you could be
Capable of,
You will never
Grow.
- Belle Doyle (137)

Demon Eyes

Oh darling don't you realize
The only reason you tripped
Was because you believed
The trees had eyes.
The only reason you fumbled
Was because you believed
The stones had ears.
Oh darling imagine
What you could do
If you stopped believing
The sun was a spy.
- Belle Doyle (138)

World of Roses

The world wishes to always
Be a rose.
Has admired it's vivid colour,
Protective thorns,
And it's consistent beauty
From the moment
It blooms
To the moment
It wilts.
Yet she wished
To be a dandelion
Capable of
Beautiful and powerful
Change.
- Belle Doyle (167)

Brothers' Love

Leather and horse hoof
Smelling truck
Driving as fast as your grandpa,
It's a dark night,
Not a star nor light in sight
Until we reach city limits.
Melody soothing so loud,
My band-aid covered heart
Quakes to the country tune.
Guitar twine and simple jokes
Rock this heart whole for just a moment.
My brothers' love
Is something so few may understand,
How lucky can I be?
They could give the distance
And cold-shoulder
Our many years apart
Suggest they should,
And yet on this dark night
Not a star nor city light in sight,
Melody soothing so loud,
I know I'll always
Be safe.
- Belle Doyle (158)

Moon Girl

I have met many suns.
Those who rant endlessly
About all they do
And all they see,
To the point you ponder,
"If I wonder away... will they notice?"
Sometimes they can
In an endless and suffocating stream of
"Where are you? I need to talk to you!"
They are bright and sometimes caring,
But in the end,
They did nothing for my soul,
Though now I think I have found a moon.
She has kind eyes
And a warm smile.
She talks of her splendor
But also her grievances.
She lets me see her
In a lens I have not seen many...
Truthfully.
She does not plow over me and my words
But pauses and listens.
I have laughed with her
Like I haven't in a while.
Above all, she does not hold me
To expectations.
I am me and that
Is enough for her.
A black cat

Who crosses your path
And lingers
Until she deems you whole.
Moon girl
You are saving my soul.
Do not fret for this
To be a one-way street,
For I hear you too
And I hope I can
Heal your soul as well.
- Belle Doyle (35)

Other Girls

The myth one tells themselves
To be able to slip beneath the
Veil of consciousness of sleep,
"I'm not like other girls." Ha.
You mean to separate yourself
From the cliches
That copy each other's every mimic
But these girls are nothing alike.
For beneath the
Fake eyelashes,
Lululemon leggings,
Long manicured nails,
And fake smiles,
Are beautiful minds,
Begging
To be released from
It's own insecurity.
- Belle Doyle (160)

Fathers

There are fathers
Who run and leave you
To die.
There are fathers
Who believe themselves to be
Tyrannical kings
And beat you down.
There are fathers
Who are present
Yet do not know
Your birthday.
The world only shows
The worst of all fathers
That boys wish
They never become
Until the cycle
Repeats.
But there is always one
To break free
And become a
Dad.
A man who
Would spend his every penny
To see you smile,
Who goes ruby-red in the head
At the simplest of jokes.
Who loves his daughter
No matter her age.
Who care to hear your

Every emotion and problem.
Who may have the maturity
Of a twelve year old,
But has wisdom beyond his days.
A true man to fill the role
That any child
Should be proud
To call
Dad.
- Belle Doyle (119)

Intuition

I swear she knows.
I swear my mother knows
When life has decided
To see how hard
It can push
Down
And
Down
Upon my shoulders
Before I buckle.
I swear she knows
When I refuse to let
My chin drop,
And a tear slip.
I swear she know
As soon as my eyes
Burn
And my throat
Seizes.
I swear she knows
No matter how far apart we are,
For when my
World is collapsing
Whilst a smile is on my face,
I see a text
Telling me
I'm okay.
- Belle Doyle (47)

Recipe For Solace

Music and poetry.
The recipe of happiness.
Under a tree
On a sunny day.
In a classroom
Avoiding work, and reality itself.
Laying in bed
With the moon for light
And dreams beckoning you
To sleep.
Anytime.
Anywhere.
Music and poetry
Offer solace to this
Healing soul.
- Belle Doyle (46)

Coming Home

The road to pure
Joy,
Happiness,
And curiosity,
No longer seems far
And without as many disturbances.
Thought there's more to learn still,
The aches and festering anxieties
Are healing and letting go.
And though this feeling
Could be temporary
As most things are,
Hopefully the feeling
Of coming home to myself
Shall last.
- Belle Doyle (30)

Compressional Societal Expectations

Some crave
Everyday repetition
With little change
That could give their heart a flutter,
Some crave
Pure freedom
Changing day by day
Never to know the meaning of
'Settle down'.
But I cannot stand either
On full force.
I love everyday repetition
And it's comfort
But waking up at the same time,
Completing the same work,
Eating the same food,
Dreaming the same dreary dreams,
Day
By
Day
Becomes so
Dry
And lacks real life.
And yet having nothing
To tie your feet to the ground
And keep your mind
From drifting far beyond
The clouds
Is dangerous;

A lifestyle begging for failure,
Doomed to default to boredom.
For once there is nothing left to explore
Nothing left to say,
Nothing left to learn,
Nothing left to teach,
Nothing left to do,
I'd find myself begging
To have the ties
I'd chewed apart
With my own
Immature ignorance.
Despite your attempts
To sway me to a or b.
I ask
Why not have both?
I'd rather
Learn balance
Among my heart and soul
Than lose my soul
By choosing between
Society's predetermined paths.
- Belle Doyle (146)

Save Yourself

This world separates
Strength and beauty
Like witches and princesses,
But can't they go hand in hand?
Belle saved the beast.
Mulan protected her people.
Rapunzel made her dream come true,
Maleficent was quite misunderstood,
Witches were seen as
Ugly and horrible
Simply for the power they wielded.
So I tell you, princess,
As you wait for your
White knight in shining armor
To slay the dragon
Beneath your window,
Do it yourself,
In a dress and sparkling heels.
- Belle Doyle (62)

Red-Eyed Girl

When I see a girl
With red eyes and puffy cheeks
But when you ask
"Are you okay?"
She forces a smile and says
"I'm fine, thanks."
My heart leaps for her.
For I was her.
I am her.
And it is a scary and dangerous place
When you say
Nothing
At
All.
So I tell you
Red-eyed girl
It is okay
To not be
Okay.
- Belle Doyle (56)

Wild Mind

You say
"I don't understand what goes on in my head,"
But I think you do
And say it as an excuse.
I think you are so scared to say
"This is me!"
And default to demonizing
Your perfect personality.
Can you truly believe
No one
Will understand those unbalanced and amusing thoughts?
If you let loose your
Wild mind,
Maybe I'll let mine
Out too.
- Belle Doyle (34)

Deserved

Oh little girl,
Oh little girl,
When will you learn
To trust yourself
Instead of putting yourself so
Entirely in the hands of others?
When will you learn
To harden to the words of others
As so many have?
I envy your
Patience and hope
In humanity
But is it truly deserved?
- Belle Doyle (71)

Impact

You are a mere speck
In this unlimited universe.
Make an impact
as if
you were
a God.
- Belle Doyle (84)

Inside Out

Om the outside...
Earbuds in,
Bright-as-can-be eyes,
Hair done,
Full face of makeup,
Cheerful smile,
Little waves,
Great grades,
Oversharing,
Not sharing anything at all,
Make you laugh,
Nose in a book,
Pencil flying across a page,
Considerate words,
Spewing appreciation,
Gaining trust and respect,
All on the outside...
But on the inside?
Healing scabs,
Frozen feet,
Long mornings,
Ignored alarms,
Procrastination,
Pessimism,
Ordinary,
Struggling grades,
Venting words,
Dusty books,
Reaching out,

Locking down,
All coddled inside.
But inside out?
New-found talent,
Tendrils of trust,
Forming faith in friends,
Sharing expression
And experience,
Decent grades,
Building blocks of confidence,
All inside out.
- Belle Doyle (83)

How The Mighty Fall

Oh anxiety I laugh at your failed attempts
To hinder my success,
My dreams,
My growth.
For finally mighty anxiety,
There is no reason,
No roadblocks
To stop me from
Gambling
My
Heart
Away.
- Belle Doyle (88)

Immortal

I am not immortal
In the sense I shall live forever,
My skin never crease,
My hair forever dirty brown.
I am immortal
In the sense that
No matter what the universe
Throws my way,
I will always
Overcome
And
Breathe for another day.
- Belle Doyle (110)

Repetition of Trauma

The hammer falls
Upon your hand
So many times
One would think
You'd grow
To either
Accept and anticipate
Or learn to prevent
The next drop
And yet you
Shy away in place
And scream all the more.
It does not matter
How many times
One experiences pain
It is still
Pain
Nonetheless.
- Belle Doyle (140)

Yesterdays, Tomorrows, and Today

Yesterdays are
Irreversible,
Usually unforgettable,
Filled with memories
Or regret,
And everything
In between.
Tomorrows are
Filled with hopes and dreads,
Worry and excitement,
Everchanging,
Undecided,
And everything
In between.
But today?
Today is lost.
Lost in the mind
Of those stuck
In the past
And future.
Lost to those who
Are too caught up
In what was
And what could be.

- Belle Doyle (54)

Born or Made

What makes a poet?
It is not
Perfectly curated words
Nor a sharp tongue and mind,
But an ability to
Purely feel.
What makes a poet?
It is not
A readers nose and
A mind powered by caffeine,
But a hyperawareness
To catch even the smallest
Twitch of an eye
Or a word not yet
Graced the space.
What makes a poet?
It is not
A skill of writing
Nor an extroverted task,
But the ability to
Understand oneself
So entirely
And yet,
Not understand
A thing
About the world.
- Belle Doyle (179)

Part 3:
Spreading Growth

Empty Gods

"Money can't buy happiness"
But it can be the
Stepping stones of savory,
Aided by praise and esteem
To raise the selfish to glory.
Tear away at dread
To replace with fulfilled dreams.
Acolytes gathering at their feet,
Riches in tow.
Creating
Empty gods
With
Empty heads.
Void of feeling.
Void of truth.
- Belle Doyle (21)

Memento Mori

Memento mori
Remember you will die.
Adventurers use it
As an excuse
To do everything they can.
Overthinkers use it
As an excuse
To do nothing at all.
- Belle Doyle (80)

Run Boy

Run little boy,
Run fast and hard,
With your stolen bride
Who leaves skids in the mud beneath,
And screams under your grasp.
Run little boy,
Run from fate's timer and decided path.
Run from karma's harsh noose.
Run little boy, run.
But do not forget,
That decisive duo,
Will always be at your side
In the blink of an unexpected eye.
- Belle Doyle (95)

Run Girl

Run little girl,
Run fast and hard
Through thick-thorned lush,
From the iron fist of responsibility,
And the leash of man.
Run little girl,
Run into karma's cool comfort,
And Hecate's feminine rage for justice.
Run little girl, run.
Run like you've never ran before.
Run until your name is unknown.
But do not forget,
To be lost
Is to be forever
Alone,
In a world that
Denies all you are.
- Belle Doyle (113)

Pyres

Upon the pyre
With flames colouring
Her legs
And burning her skirt
To smithereens,
She did not twitch,
She did not scream,
She did not cry,
She merely looked
Her violators in their
Deceiving eyes and only said
"I shall rise again."
Upon the pyre
In a country that
Blasts freedom
With flames burning away
Her freedom of choice,
Oh she writhed,
And oh she cried.
She stared down her violators
Who voted away her
Choice over her own anatomy,
And spoke with a severity
That chilled all who heard
To the bone
And said
"I shall rise again."
- Belle Doyle (147)

Subconscious Hauntings

People are haunted
Each day
With ghosts on their heels
And latched onto their mind.
But not your
Traditional ghosts
Who wish to
Resolve their life's pain.
No.
These ghosts are the
Hauntings of our subconscious
We formulate in dark corners
And believe whisper
In our ear.
We become so obsessed
With the next whisper,
The next shift,
The next incident,
We miss our lives,
And slowly slip
Into absolute
Insanity.
- Belle Doyle (133)

Influence Yourself

How sad a life
To follow in the
Flock of sheep
Who all hide their
Black wool
In white paint
And criticize when another
Bleeds gray.
How sad a life
To allow the masses
To influence your every move.
How sad a life
To not know your
Own mind
But every
Whim and wish
Of another who
Doesn't even care
To know your name.
- Belle Doyle (143)

Addict

You always say
"I'll never be one of those obsessed people."
When a red-eyed,
Foaming mouthed,
Addicted person
Raves about how
Amazing their substance is
And all they can do.
You try your best to
Resist the temptation of horror,
But on a day so empty
With not even a cloud
To imagine a friend
You say to yourself
"Once won't hurt"
You lay your greedy hands upon the
Unforgiving substance
And take a small taste.
Oh what a mistake.
You are sucked into a world of
White lies,
Pretty smiles,
And make-up concealed hate.
You were instantly turned off from
The hidden horrors wrapped
In a laugh.
Though the very next day
You say
"Once more shall do no harm... right?"

Oh only if you realized sooner.
The hours slipped by,
Your eyes glazed over,
Your lips dried,
And your stomach rumbled.
In one taste the
Spiderweb woven by
Social media had you snared.
Some lines of silk
Demeaned you,
Scared you,
Stabbed you,
Complimented you,
Confused you,
Made you laugh,
Made you cry,
Made you mad.
You tried to quit,
To escape the claws
Entrenched in your mind.
You tried for a day,
A week,
And sometimes even
A month
But you'd go crawling
Back,
Acting as though
You'd lost your soul.
Your back began to hunch,
Your skin lost it's lush colour,
Your eyes reddened,
And your mouth began to foam.
You wandered aimless trying
To get your next fix.
You spewed it's wonders

To any you laid eyes on,
Trying to turn them,
Convince them,
To become an
Addict
Just
Like
You.
- Belle Doyle (141)

Flatline

Heartbeat and heart thrums
Up and down
Sloshing blood
Pounding through
Crimson veins
Racing hard,
Before the next batch
Makes it's match.
Without the highs
And without the lows
Of your
Heartbeat and heart thrums,
You'd greet the grim reaper
Upon a flatline,
And yet a
Flatline life
Is all
You beg for.
- Belle Doyle (153)

They're Coming For You

Poor innocent girl
Twirling and giggling
In pure, unashamed freedom
Existing just as you are.
The world sits and awaits
The verdict of your trial
To see who
Must hate you,
Must love you,
Must worship you,
Must deceive you.
They're coming for you,
Innocent strong girl.
Don't be afraid,
They once came for me too.
They're coming for you
In their white lab coats
And clipboards that are
Filled to the brim
With little boxes
Waiting for you to fill them up.
They're coming for you.
They ask you every
Question under the sun
Until your mind blends
Round and round
Into a drowsed stupor,
Ticking boxes as they go.
They came for you

And their brows knit together
As they all whisper
"impossible"
Their voices lower
And their pens race.
Oh innocent girl,
You may start a riot.
They don't understand
And neither does the world.
A panic erupts
As we've all been told
We must.
Conspiracies fly.
Some believe that
You're arrival must mean
The world's end.
Some believe that
You're the devil's
Incarnation.
Hunting parties form,
Only held back by the word
Of the all ruling
Lab coats.
"You don't fit in."
Oh innocent girl.
The world shrieks and panics
You've begun to cry,
But darling look out the window
To earth is just the same
As it was
Before they came for you.
No lava spews.
No cracks have splintered.
No flames erupted.
You don't fit into the

Lifeless mass called society
And yet the world
Does not stop spinning.
So innocent girl
Wipe your cheeks,
Smile that same
Pure and free smile
And know
Being you
Is the best
There is
In a
Black and white
World
That was finally
Graced with colour.
- Belle Doyle (164)

Flowers

You wish to die
For you believe there is
No one left
In your life
And yet
There will still be
Flowers at your grave.
You wish to die
For you believe
You are not worthy
Of a beating heart
And yet
There will still be
Flowers at your grave
That disagree.
You wish to die
For you no longer
Love yourself
And believe no love
Is spared for your breath
And yet
There will still be
Flowers at your grave
With hearts attached.
You wish to die
And yet
There will still be
Flowers at your grave
Giving you every

Reason
To keep
Breathing.
- Belle Doyle (165)

People Are Ugly

Saying the repeated and tired line
"this world is an ugly place"
Is benign and simply a lie.
For the world itself
And it's sprawling forests,
Unknown oceans,
Powerful mountains,
Rolling hills,
Blue skies,
And sparkling stars,
Begs to disagree.
Rather it is the people who
Choke out the atmosphere,
Burn it's forests,
Destroy it's lush land,
Decimate oceans,
They don't even understand,
That are the ugly creatures.
So instead of saying
Mother Earth
And all her glory
Is ugly and grave,
Say
"We humans are hideous."
- Belle Doyle (169

Seek Out

Some people seek
Happiness.
Some people seek
Anger.
Some people seek
Jealousy.
Some people seek
Freedom.
And some people seek
Sorrow.
They seek out sorrow
As though it is
The last droplet of water
Upon the Earth's crust.
They seek sorrow
For it's cutting comfort.
They seek out sorrow
For after having a heart
So fully drenched
In it's silky lies,
One may never understand
The warm light
Of happiness
Again.
- Belle Doyle (171)

Innocence

As time rages,
It seems as though
Each generation is losing
It's innocence.
For since when
Were toys tossed away
For a womanly glam
Before a girl reaches
Ten?
It seems as though
The time for justice clothes
and joys
Become smaller
And smaller.
Even when I,
Hide behind
A face full of makeup,
I fear for those
Younger than me
As their youthful innocence
Is stolen at a
Younger
And younger
Age.
- Belle Doyle (40)

Welcoming Death

As the world evolves,
It's happiness deteriorates.
It seems as though the newer the generation,
The sadder they are.
Older generations were
Friends with life
And fear death.
It seems as though
The younger,
The more stress,
The more sadness,
The closer they are
To welcoming death
Over life.
- Belle Doyle (41)

Puzzled Hurricane

"If only you knew the beginning of it,"
She said as the
Bright in her eye
Dimmed ever-so-slightly
One would need
A heart of gold
To see it.
"Do you even know?"
He asked,
Feeling as though
He were a sea
Away from her.
"No, no I do not."
- Belle Doyle (105)

Letters to Men

Dear men,
We are not your
Toys,
Caretakers,
Dolls,
Servants,
Trophies,
Slaves,
You believe us to be.
Nor are you
Masters,
Kings,
Dominant,
All-knowing,
Infantile,
You believe yourself to be.
Sincerely,
A fifteen-year-old female poet.
Dear men,
How can you truly
Believe us meek

In the 21st century?
Our brains are
Quite similar
And capable of strong decision making
Yet you say we are murderers
In the name of religion
Under the wish of control
Even though

Your own gods handbooks
Says life begins
At first breath.
Sincerely,
My body, my choice, never yours.
Dear men,
You've let the fact
Eve was made for
Adam
Go straight to your head.
You even believe she
Was his property,
Created for his enjoyment.
But I would bet
Eve was created
To save Adam
From his own incompetence.
Sincerely,
Female business owner.
- Belle Doyle (123)

Effect of Words

A misconception
So many believe
About beautiful poetry,
Is these words do not
Have to rhyme
As long as the
Meaning is strong enough
To bring mountains
To their knees,
Slow roaring rivers
To a sweet stream
And move millions
Of relating hearts.
- Belle Doyle (131)

9 798223 768852